A Note to Parents & Teachers—

Welcome to I See Animals from Xist Publishing! These books are designed to inspire discovery and delight in the youngest readers. Each book features very simple sentences with visual cues to help beginners read their very first text.

You can help each child develop a lifetime love of reading right from the very start. Here are some ways to help a beginning reader get going:

 Read the book aloud as a first introduction

 Run your fingers below the words as you read each line

 Give the child the chance to finish the sentences or read repeating words while you read the rest.

 Encourage the child to read aloud every day!

Published in the United States by
Xist Publishing
www.xistpublishing.com
24200 Southwest Freeway
Suite 402-290
Rosenberg, TX 77471

eISBN: 978-1-5324-1405-3
Saddle Stitch ISBN: 978-1-5324-1476-3
Perfect Bound ISBN: 978-1-5324-4198-1
Hardcover ISBN: 978-1-5324-3395-5

© 2020 by Xist Publishing
All rights reserved
No portion of this book may be reproduced without express permission of the publisher
All images licensed from Adobe Stock
First Edition

I See Animals
Chipmunk

written by August Hoeft

INSPIRING DISCOVERY & DELIGHT

I see a chipmunk.

The chipmunk has black stripes.

The chipmunk has big cheeks.

The chipmunk eats seeds.

The chipmunk lives in the forest.

I see a chipmunk.

Things to do next!

Write a Sentence

I see a _____.

Drawing

Make a drawing of your favorite animal.

Sharing

Talk to your classmates about your favorite picture in this book. Explain to them why you like it.

WORD LIST

a	has
big	I
black	in
cheeks	is
chipmunk	see
eats	seeds
forest	stripes
lives	the

Have you read the other I See Animals Books?

Alligator	Giraffe	Panda
Bear	Goat	Parrot
Beaver	Gorilla	Penguin
Butterfly	Guinea Pig	Pig
Cat	Hamster	Polar Bear
Cheetah	Hedgehog	Puppy
Chicken	Hippo	Rabbit
Chinchilla	Horse	Raccoon
Chipmunk	Jellyfish	Rhino
Cow	Kangaroo	Sea Lion
Deer	Kitten	Sea Turtle
Dog	Lemur	Shark
Dolphin	Lion	Sheep
Donkey	Lizard	Snail
Duck	Llama	Snake
Eagle	Love Bird	Squirrel
Elephant	Meerkat	Squirrel Monkey
Elk	Monkey	Tiger
Ferret	Moose	Tree Frog
Fish	Mountain Lion	Turkey
Fox	Mouse	Turtle
Frog	Octopus	Whale
Giant Panda	Orca	Wolf
Giant Tortoise	Owl	Zebra